☆ ☆ ☆

Ronald Reagan

Ronald Reagan

Kieran Doherty

AMERICA'S **40**TH PRESIDENT

Children's Press®
A Division of Scholastic Inc.
New York / Toronto / London / Auckland / Sydney
Mexico City / New Delhi / Hong Kong
Danbury, Connecticut

Library of Congress Cataloging-in-Publication Data

Doherty, Kieran.
        Ronald Reagan / Kieran Doherty.
            p. cm. — (Encyclopedia of presidents. Second series)
Includes bibliographical references and index.
    ISBN 0-516-22979-6
    1. Reagan, Ronald—Juvenile literature. 2. Presidents—United States—
Biography—Juvenile literature. I. Title. II. Encyclopedia of presidents (2003)
E877.D64 2005
973.927'092—dc22   2004024065

Contents

One   7
Humble Beginnings

Two   21
The Birth of a Politician

Three   35
The Road to Washington

Four   51
First Term

Five   65
Second Term

Six   85
Into the Sunset

Presidential Fast Facts   96
First Lady Fast Facts   97
Timeline   98
Glossary   100
Further Reading   101
Places to Visit   102
Online Sites of Interest   103
Table of Presidents   104
Index   108

Chapter 1

President in Danger

On the afternoon of March 30, 1981, only two months after Ronald Reagan was sworn in as president, he spoke to a group of union leaders at a hotel in Washington, D.C. After speaking, Reagan came out of the double doors of the hotel. As he walked toward his waiting limousine, he stopped to wave at some supporters who were cheering him from across the street.

Just then, to the president's left, a 25-year-old college dropout named John Hinckley Jr. stepped forward with a small handgun. Before anybody could act, Hinckley fired six shots in quick succession. One of the bullets, a type designed to do maximum damage inside a victim's body, bounced off the president's limousine and tore into Reagan's chest beneath his upraised arm.

Ronald Reagan waves to supporters outside the Washington Hilton Hotel only moments before being shot and seriously wounded by an assassin.

The assassination attempt might have ended Reagan's presidency almost before it began, but he was fortunate. Although the bullet wounded him gravely, he recovered fully and went on to serve eight years as president. In those years, Ronald Reagan earned a place in history as one of the most important—and controversial—presidents in history.

Birth and Early Life

Ronald Reagan was born in the small town of Tampico, in northern Illinois, on February 6, 1911. His father, John Edward Reagan, was a shoe salesman. His mother, Nelle Wilson Reagan, was a woman of strong religious beliefs who devoted much of her life to doing charitable works for neighbors. Ronald was their second son. Their older boy, Neil, was born in 1908.

A picture of Ronald Reagan taken when he was one year old shows that he was a plump baby. John Reagan thought his baby son looked just like "a fat little Dutchman," so Ronald got the nickname "Dutch."

In Tampico, a town of about 1,000 people, the Reagan family lived in a cramped apartment over a general store. The family had little money. John Reagan was an alcoholic. When he was not drinking alcohol, he would work hard and provide for his family. Then, without warning, he would begin drinking and

The Reagan family about 1915. Ronald (right center) is about four years old.

stay drunk for a week or two at a time. As a result of his drinking, he lost good jobs and fell far behind in paying his bills, but he never stopped trying to take care of his wife and children. He traveled from town to town in search of jobs and when he worked, he supported his family as well as he could.

Though the family was poor, Reagan would later say he did not feel deprived as a child. "I suppose we were poor," he said, "but we never knew we were poor."

Neil Reagan had different memories. He remembered sharing one bed with Ronald and going to a butcher shop to ask for a ten-cent soup bone and for liver for a cat that the family did not have. "Our big meal on Sunday was always fried liver," he recalled. "We ate on the soup bone all the rest of the week."

High School

When Dutch Reagan was nine, the family moved to Dixon, a somewhat larger town about 20 miles (32 kilometers) from Tampico. He finished elementary school there and graduated from Dixon Northside High School. He always called Dixon his hometown.

Dutch Reagan was not a good student, but he was very eager when it came to sports, especially football. Though he was small, he tried out for the Dixon High football team and kept trying until he finally made the squad in his third year. By his

DOROTHY RANDALL
"*An A-1 student, the teacher's joy.*"
Gym 2, 3; Cinean Lit. 1, 2; Joyce
Kilmer 3, 4; Play 3; Annual Staff.

DONALD REAGAN
"Dutch"
"*Life is just one grand sweet song,
so start the music.*"
Pres. N. S. Student Body 4; Pres.
2; Play 3, 4; Dram. Club 3, 4, Pres.
4; Fresh.-Soph. Drama Club 1, 2,
Pres. 2; Football 3, 4; Annual Staff;
Hi-Y 3, 4, Vice-Pres. 4; Art. 1, 2;
Lit. Contest 2; Track 2, 3.

1928

The entry for Ronald Reagan in his high school yearbook in 1928. He is mistakenly identified as "Donald."

senior season, he had grown about 6 inches (15 centimeters) and gained 30 pounds (13.6 kilograms), and was big enough to earn a spot as a starter on the team.

Reagan's mother enjoyed performing. She gave dramatic readings for social clubs and for hospital patients. She introduced her son to acting. By the time he was a senior in high school, he was tall and good-looking, and was a popular young man with his classmates. He joined the school drama society and played the lead in a school play.

In addition to playing football in his senior year, Dutch Reagan also played basketball and ran on the track team. He was elected president of the student body. When the senior class yearbook was published, the motto under his class photo read, "Life is just one sweet song, so let the music begin." This was a line from a long, rather sweet poem Reagan had written earlier.

College Days

After graduating from high school in 1928, Reagan enrolled at Eureka College in central Illinois. His family could not afford to pay his tuition and room and board, so Dutch went to work to earn his own way. Jack Reagan had instilled in his sons his belief that anyone could conquer the world through hard work. It was a belief that shaped much of Ronald Reagan's life.

Reagan had already begun to work during his summer vacations in high school. One summer, he got a job digging the foundation at a local construction site. The pay was 25 cents an hour (not bad for the times), and the work made him stronger for sports. He also got a job as a lifeguard at a nearby lake. He returned to that job for six summers in a row. In later life, Reagan spoke often of his summers as a lifeguard, during which he claimed to have saved more than 75 lives. Once he also "rescued" a swimmer's false teeth, and received a $10 tip for his services.

By the fall of 1928, Reagan had saved $400, enough to pay for his tuition, food, and lodging for a whole school year. He also had a girlfriend, Margaret

Reagan as a lifeguard. He worked at the Lowell Park Beach in Dixon for seven summers through high school and college.

Ronald Reagan was always grateful to Eureka College for the happy days he spent there. Years later, when he was running for president, he visited the college. "Everything good that has happened to me—everything— started here on this campus," he said.

☆ ☆ ☆

Cleaver, called "Mugs" by her friends. She was the daughter of a local minister in Dixon and one of Dutch's high school classmates. She and Reagan had acted together in a school play and soon started to date. Like Dutch Reagan, Mugs Cleaver was about to enroll at Eureka College.

At college Ronald Reagan was only a fair student, partly because he continued to work. He relied on cramming sessions he called "quick studies" just before taking tests. Putting in just enough work to get by scholastically, he earned a C average. According to his older brother Neil, Reagan would "take a book the night before the test and in about a quick hour he would thumb through it . . . and write a good test."

Even though Reagan was no standout in his studies, he became a star outside the classroom. He joined the football, track, and swim teams, and he won a sports scholarship that paid half his tuition. He also served as editor of the school yearbook and as head of the student council. He was active in the college drama club. One of his classmates said he had a "personality that would sweep you off your feet."

The Great Depression ———————————————

By the time Reagan returned to the Eureka campus in the fall of 1930, the United States was falling into the economic crisis known as the Great Depression. The previous year, the stock market had crashed. Business activity in the United States and around the world was slowing to a crawl. Millions of Americans had lost their jobs and could not find work. In Chicago, the state's largest city, nearly half the people who wanted jobs could not find work of any kind. Conditions in Dixon were not much better.

When the Depression started, Jack Reagan had just started to find some financial success. He was the partner in a small shoe store in Dixon. As times got worse, people could no longer afford new shoes, and the shoe store, along with thousands of other businesses, was forced to close its doors. Jack Reagan was unemployed. The only money coming into the Reagan house in Dixon was the $14 a week earned by Reagan's mother, who found work as a seamstress in a dress shop. His parents were forced to rent out half of their apartment and live in a single room, cooking on a hot plate.

At Eureka, Dutch Reagan increased the hours he worked. In addition to paying his own expenses, he began sending money back to his parents to help them get through these difficult times.

Reagan on Radio

Reagan graduated from Eureka College in 1932. Since other jobs were scarce, he took his old job as a lifeguard that summer. In the fall, he decided to look for work as a radio announcer. He borrowed his father's car and visited every station within a half-day's drive of Dixon. Reagan had little or no experience that would qualify him for a radio job, but neither did anyone else. Popular radio, with news, entertainment, and music, was scarcely ten years old, but it was growing rapidly, since millions of homes had inexpensive radio receivers.

Dutch Reagan's voice was rich and strong, perfect for a career in radio. At radio station WOC in Davenport, Iowa, he was given a chance to audition as a sports announcer. His knowledge of sports and his good speaking voice won

Reagan as a young radio announcer for station WHO in Des Moines, Iowa.

him the job. Soon afterward, WOC merged with WHO, a more powerful station in Des Moines, Iowa. When Reagan broadcast from WHO, his voice reached hundreds of miles.

Reagan made his biggest impression as a play-by-play announcer of Chicago Cubs baseball games. He did not travel to Chicago or other cities, where he could actually watch the game. Instead, he sat in the WHO studios, reading telegraphed play-by-play descriptions of the game. He made up many of the details of the game himself, but listeners said they felt that they were really at the game. By the time he was 25, Reagan was a minor radio celebrity in Iowa and surrounding states.

From Radio to the Movies

In 1937 Reagan convinced his bosses to send him to California to cover the Chicago Cubs' spring training games. The team trained on Santa Catalina Island in the Pacific Ocean, just off the coast of Los Angeles. During the trip, Reagan met Joy Hodges, a Des Moines native who was working as a singer and actress in Hollywood, the section of Los Angeles where the movie business had its studios. Eventually, Hodges arranged for Reagan to meet her agent, Bill Meiklejohn.

Meiklejohn ran an agency that represented some of the biggest stars in Hollywood, and he liked Reagan's appearance, his pleasing voice, and his confident manner. He called Warner Brothers, one of the leading movie studios, to set up a screen test. Reagan took the test, but he could not wait around to learn the results. He had to return to work in Des Moines.

A week later, Meiklejohn sent Reagan a telegram. It reported that Warner Brothers was offering a contract that would pay him $200 a week to make movies and it asked what Reagan wanted to do. In the middle of the Depression, $200 a week was a princely sum. Reagan had no doubts. He sent a quick telegram reply: "Sign before they change their minds."

Chapter 2

Hollywood Success

Ronald Reagan was soon a successful and prosperous movie actor in Hollywood. While most aspiring actors waited months or even years before they got a decent part, Reagan was working in front of a camera within a week of his arrival. His very first role seemed to be made just for him. He played the part of a radio announcer in *Love Is on the Air*. He was a "good guy" who tricks some crooks into admitting into an open microphone that they committed a murder.

Over the next several years, Reagan appeared mostly in what were known as "B" movies. These were low-budget films without major Hollywood stars. On occasion, he had a part in an "A" movie. One such movie was *Dark Victory*, with leading lady Bette Davis. Still, Reagan had no illusions about his work. Commenting about the "B" pictures he played in, he remarked, that the producers "don't want them good, they want them Thursday."

In 1940, three years after he arrived in Hollywood, Reagan gained wide attention and praise for his role as football player George Gipp in *Knute Rockne All American*, a movie about the famous football coach at Notre Dame University. Gipp was a star on one of Rockne's Notre Dame teams who died of pneumonia while still in college. In his deathbed scene, Reagan urges the coach to ask his team to "win one for the Gipper."

Forty years later, when Reagan was running for president, millions of sports and movie fans still remembered Reagan's role as the Gipper. Reagan's critics could point to his less-inspired movie roles. One was *Bedtime for Bonzo* (1951), in which Reagan played a professor who was trying to teach Bonzo, a chimpanzee, to tell the difference between right and wrong.

Reagan never gained a reputation as a great film actor, but he did find regular work and financial success. At the height of his movie career, he was being paid $3,500 a week, more than factory workers at the time earned in a whole year. In all, he made more than 50 movies between 1937 and 1957.

A Storybook Marriage

In 1938, his second year in Hollywood, Reagan met actress Jane Wyman when both of them had parts in the movie *Brother Rat*. Reagan was 26 years old and Wyman was 23. Over the next few years a romance developed. The couple were

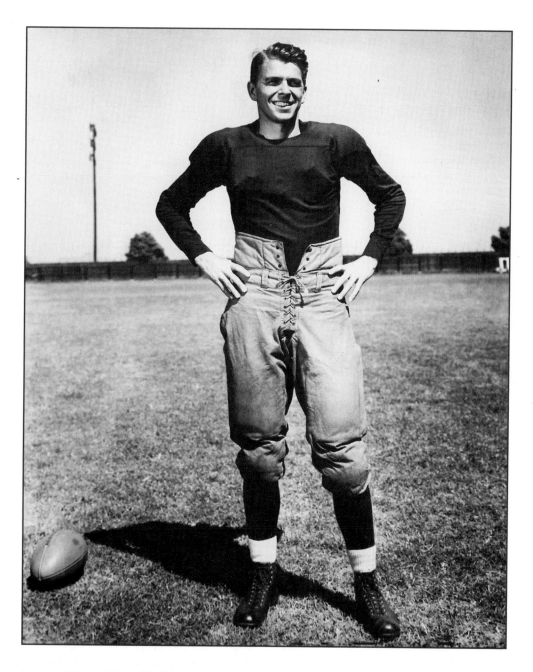

Reagan in Hollywood, dressed for the role of Notre Dame football star George Gipp in *Knute Rockne All American*. When Gipp is near death in the movie, he urges coach Rockne to ask the team one day to "win one for the Gipper."

Jane Wyman was born Sarah Jane Fulks on January 4, 1914, in St. Joseph, Missouri. Encouraged by her mother, Wyman had appeared in bit roles in Hollywood as a teenager. After attending the University of Missouri briefly, she moved to Hollywood. By 1938, when she met Ronald Reagan, she had graduated to featured roles.

Where Reagan was never considered a serious actor, Jane Wyman was. In 1948 she won the Academy Award as best actress for her performance in *Johnny Belinda*. She later became a successful television actress, winning four Golden Globe awards.

Ronald Reagan and actress Jane Wyman in 1940, a few weeks before their marriage.

spotted at famous nightclubs and mentioned together in gossip columns. By the end of 1939, they were engaged, and in January 1940 they were married.

To outsiders, Ronald Reagan and Jane Wyman seemed to have a storybook romance and marriage. They were both young and attractive and were living what most people considered a dream life. Movie magazines in the 1940s named them "Hollywood's happiest couple." On January 4, 1941, Jane gave birth to a daughter, Maureen.

Late in 1941, the U.S. military bases in Pearl Harbor, Hawaii, were attacked by Japanese bombers, and nearly 2,400 service-men were killed. The next day, the United States declared war on Japan and entered World War II. For nearly four years, the war effort became a major concern for the country and for the movie industry. Ronald Reagan was called up for service in 1942 and spent the war years making training films for the army.

Communism

Like all studio actors, Ronald Reagan joined the Screen Actors Guild (SAG) when he arrived in Hollywood in 1937. SAG was a *union* that represented film actors in negotiations with studios about pay and working conditions. Both before and after his war service, he was a member of SAG's board of

Fast Facts

WORLD WAR II

Who: The Axis powers (Germany, Japan, and Italy) against the Allies (including Great Britain, France, the Soviet Union, and later the United States)

Why: The Axis had invaded neighboring countries and were seeking world domination; the Allied powers went to war to end the aggression.

When: Began September 1, 1939, when Germany invaded Poland; the U.S. entered the war in December 1941 after Japan attacked Pearl Harbor. Germany surrendered in May 1945, and Japan surrendered on August 14, 1945.

Where: In Europe, North Africa, Asia, the Pacific Islands, and the world's oceans

Outcome: Italy surrendered in 1943; Germany surrendered May 7, 1945, as Soviet and Western European armies captured Berlin, the German capital; Japan surrendered August 14, 1945, after the U.S. dropped atomic bombs on two Japanese cities. Allied forces occupied both Germany and Japan, and the United Nations was established to help preserve peace in the future.

directors, and in 1947 he was elected its president. He was soon involved in a major fight within the group.

During the 1930s, some unions came under the influence of *Communists*, people who favored government ownership of businesses and property. These Communist-led unions hoped to extend Communist influence to other unions. As president of SAG, Reagan learned that a small group of its members were working to gain influence for the Communist party among workers in the movie industry.

At first, Reagan tried to work out a peaceful compromise between those who opposed Communism and those who favored it. He soon learned, however, that the Communist supporters did not keep their promises and that they would use threats and violence to get their way. When Reagan's own family was threatened, he began to carry a gun to protect himself.

Meanwhile, in Washington, a congressional committee popularly known as HUAC (the House Un-American Activities Committee) began an investigation of Communist influence in Hollywood. In the fall of 1947, Reagan was invited to testify. Reagan expressed strong opposition to Communism and described some of the conflicts he had faced with the pro-Communist union leaders in Hollywood.

HUAC itself used strong-arm tactics to persuade witnesses to identify present or former Communists among their friends and associates. Committee members demanded that witnesses "name names." Those who refused might find

As president of the Screen Actors Guild, Reagan testifies in 1947 before the House Un-American Activities Committee in Washington.

themselves sentenced to jail for contempt of Congress. More likely, they would find themselves on the *blacklist*, a list of supposed disloyal Americans whom movie studios would no longer hire.

Reagan was not asked to name names during his public testimony. Years later, however, biographers discovered evidence that he had been providing information on possible Communists in Hollywood to the FBI.

Divorce

Reagan's growing involvement in the Screen Actors Guild and Jane Wyman's busy film career kept husband and wife apart a great deal. In addition to their daughter Maureen, they had adopted a son, Michael, in 1945, so they were also faced with caring for two small children.

Late in 1947, Jane Wyman revealed to the Hollywood press that she and Ronald Reagan had separated. The following year she filed for divorce. In hearings, she testified that Reagan seemed so preoccupied with his union activities that he had become detached from his family. "Finally there was nothing in common between us," she said. The judge granted her request, and the end of the marriage was made official in 1949.

Reagan did not contest the divorce, but his friends at the time testified that he was deeply unhappy about it. Years later, he said, "Maybe I should have let someone else save the world and saved my own home."

Nancy Davis

In 1951, an actress named Nancy Davis asked for Reagan's help. She was being confused with another actress with a similar name who was said to be a Communist sympathizer. She hoped that the president of the actors' union could help end the confusion. Reagan did straighten out the matter, and he met with Nancy Davis to give her the good news.

By early 1952, Reagan and Davis were engaged, and they were married on March 4 at a small chapel in Hollywood. The actor William Holden served as Reagan's best man, and Holden's wife Ardis was Nancy's matron of honor. Reagan later said that Nancy was the best thing that ever happened to him: "It is almost impossible for me to express fully how deeply I love Nancy and how much she has filled my life."

Television

Reagan's career took a turn in 1954 when he was given the opportunity to host a weekly television program, the *General Electric Theater*. The job required appearing as the program's host each week and acting in one or two of the productions each season. The show proved to be a popular one, appearing on Sunday nights to large audiences. Reagan served as its host for eight seasons. His weekly "visits" on television screens in living rooms across America made his face and name known to millions of people.

In addition, Reagan acted as General Electric's company spokesman. In this role, he visited GE plants around the country, making speeches to boost

Reagan and Nancy Davis (second from right) on their wedding day in 1952. They are celebrating with actor William Holden (right) and his wife Ardis (also known as Brenda Marshall, left).

company morale. At first, Reagan talked about television and Hollywood. As his audience grew, he began talking about the dangers of political issues such as waste in government. By Reagan's estimation, he met some 250,000 people. At the same time, he sharpened his skills as a public speaker.

Ron and Nancy Reagan had settled in a ranch-style house in Pacific Palisades, a seaside community near Los Angeles. Late in 1952, their daughter Patti was born. Nearly six years later, in 1958, they had a son, Ronald Reagan Jr.

Television personality Ronald Reagan, who served as host of the *General Electric Theater* for eight seasons.

A Conservative Politician

Reagan became a strong anti-Communist in the 1940s, but he remained a loyal Democrat. In 1948 he campaigned for the re-election of Democratic president Harry Truman. By 1952 his political views were changing. He remained a

Democrat but chose to support the Republican nominee for president, Dwight D. Eisenhower. Four years later he supported Eisenhower again.

In 1960, Reagan supported Republican candidate Richard Nixon for president, but Nixon lost a close race to Democrat John F. Kennedy. Nixon returned to California and ran for governor in 1962. By this time, Reagan had become an accomplished spokesman for conservative causes. He agreed to campaign for Nixon. That year, he officially changed his registration from Democrat to Republican. Nixon lost the election for governor to Democrat Pat Brown.

In 1964 conservatives took control of the Republican party and nominated Arizona senator Barry Goldwater for president. For this campaign, Reagan was a part of Goldwater's campaign team. As the election approached, it became clear that Goldwater would lose to President Lyndon B. Johnson by a large margin. Reagan was asked to make a last-ditch speech on national television to rally Republican support. This speech, on October 27, 1964, put Reagan on the national political stage for the first time.

The speech was a version of the one he had given for years to audiences at General Electric plants. It criticized big government and especially liberal Democrats like President Johnson, and it ended with a rousing call to action. "You and I have a rendezvous with destiny," Reagan told his audience. "We'll preserve

Reagan attends the 1964 Republican convention in San Francisco. He is showing off his ribbon supporting conservative Barry Goldwater for president.

for our children this, the last best hope of man on earth, or we'll sentence them to take the first step into a thousand years of darkness." His audience, mostly convinced Republicans, loved the speech and came to admire the speaker.

"Of course, I didn't know it then, but that speech was one of the most important milestones in my life," Reagan later said. In fact, it put him on the path that would lead first to the governor's mansion in California and then on to the White House.

Running for Governor

In 1965 a group of influential California Republicans asked Reagan to run for governor. Reagan's first response was amazement that he had been asked. "I'd never given a thought to running for office and I had no interest in it whatever," he said. For weeks, Reagan continued telling his new fans that he would not run, but eventually they wore down his resistance. He agreed to seek the governor's job if his supporters could promise that there would be adequate campaign funds and that key Republicans would support him. Assured he would get ample support, Reagan announced his intention to run for the governor's office on January 4, 1966. Nearly 55 years old, Reagan was making his first run for elective office at a fairly advanced age. Yet he soon proved to have many of the tools of an effective campaigner, thanks to his long experience as an actor and public speaker.

Reagan first faced Republican George Christopher, a former mayor of San Francisco, in a primary election to decide the Republican nominee. Christopher concentrated on attacking Reagan. One moment he accused Reagan of being too conservative to win election, then later suggested that Reagan was a Communist sympathizer. Christopher was so negative that Republican leaders publicly scolded him during the campaign. When the votes were counted, Reagan proved to be a powerful vote-getter among Republicans. He won twice as many votes as Christopher, with 1.4 million to Christopher's 700,000.

The General Election

Reagan then faced Democratic governor Edmund G. (Pat) Brown in the general election. Brown was a popular governor with an impressive record. During his years in office he had overseen the construction of the finest network of high-speed highways (known as freeways) in the nation. He had also helped build the state's widely admired university and its system of public colleges. He was also an accomplished politician and campaigner. In 1962 he had easily defeated former vice president Richard Nixon for governor.

Brown made the mistake of thinking that Reagan would be easy to beat. Instead of taking Reagan seriously, he portrayed him as a washed-up actor with no political experience and as a right-wing extremist. Instead of answering Brown's charges that he was inexperienced, Reagan turned the charge to his advantage. He agreed that he was an outsider, and presented himself as an ordinary citizen who wanted to "clean up the mess in Sacramento," the state capital.

Brown's charge that Reagan was an extremist was a little harder to shake, especially after the superconservative John Birch Society *endorsed* (officially recommended) him. Birch Society members were rabid anti-Communists who charged that many leading politicians, including former Republican president Dwight D. Eisenhower, were agents of a Communist conspiracy. Reagan

Reagan with a broom during his 1966 campaign for governor. The trash barrel says, "Help Us Clean Up the Mess in Sacramento."

accepted the Birch Society's endorsement, but he was careful to say, "They are accepting my philosophy, I'm not accepting theirs."

During the campaign, Reagan often took questions from the audience. He learned from these sessions that many voters were angry about violent student demonstrations at the University of California in Berkeley and at other state campuses. The disturbances had begun in 1964, when students were protesting limits to on-campus political activities. By 1966 the main issue was demonstrations against the Vietnam War. Reagan too had been upset by the ugly scenes on campuses, and he promised that he would take a strong stand against them.

On this issue and others, Reagan tapped into the new wave of conservatism that was sweeping the country. Riots in African American sections of many U.S. cities, including Watts (a part of Los Angeles), the growth of a new drug culture among young people, and protests against U.S. involvement in the Vietnam War made the mid-1960s a period of growing unrest. Voters looked to Reagan and other conservative candidates to restore law and order and to return the country to more traditional values.

At the same time, the Reagan campaign remained cheerful and upbeat. Reagan still had the glamorous good looks of a movie star, and he enlisted the help of some the nation's most popular entertainers, including he-man actor John Wayne, and actor-singers Frank Sinatra and Dean Martin. They made commercials backing his candidacy and sometimes performed during campaign rallies.

As the November election approached, many experts assumed that Pat Brown would beat Reagan and win another term as governor. They were wrong. Reagan beat his opponent by nearly a million votes, even carrying some of the state's traditionally Democratic districts.

After winning an upset victory over Democratic governor Pat Brown, Reagan speaks into a tangle of microphones.

Governor Reagan —————————————————————

After the election, Ronald and Nancy Reagan were guests at the most elaborate inaugural party ever staged in the state. When Nancy Reagan complained that the governor's mansion in Sacramento was too old and confining, the Reagans' supporters bought a much larger and more elegant house in Sacramento for the couple to live in.

In office for the first time, Reagan faced making good as the chief executive of the nation's most populous state. He approached the task with good humor. When a reporter asked what his first priority would be, he said, "I don't know. I've never played a governor."

Reagan gradually realized that making campaign promises was easier than keeping them. He wanted to lower taxes, but Governor Brown had committed to very expensive programs and left the state with big bills to pay. The cost of government services was sure to grow in any case, because the state's population was growing rapidly. In addition, the state legislature was controlled by Democrats, who would oppose Reagan's proposals to lower taxes and reduce spending.

During his first term, Reagan failed to keep most of his campaign promises. He did order a state hiring freeze and cut the budgets of state departments by 10 percent, but state expenditures continued to rise. In fact, during Reagan's eight years as governor, California's annual budget more than doubled, from $4.6 billion to more than $10 billion. To pay for all this, Reagan was forced to support tax increases rather than decreases. Even so, he remained popular with voters. Many believed that he was looking out for their interests, and they liked and trusted him enough to return him to office in 1970.

His second term was more successful. One of his main goals was to reduce California's welfare rolls. He believed that the state should provide assistance to people who were disabled or could not find employment, but he also thought that thousands of welfare recipients found it easier to receive government payments than to look for a job. Remembering his father's lesson that any individual who worked hard could be successful, Reagan had little sympathy for people who lacked ambition. "I just wanted to stop the abuses, take people off the welfare rolls who didn't belong there," he said. Reagan signed his welfare reform bill in 1971, soon after his re-election. The reform tightened qualifications for receiving welfare payments and required able-bodied welfare recipients to work.

Presidential Politics

In 1968 the California delegation to the Republican National Convention nominated Governor Reagan as its *favorite son* candidate for president. (A favorite son is placed in nomination by delegates from his home state as a sign of respect.) Richard M. Nixon received the presidential nomination on the first ballot, but Reagan gained a few minutes in the national spotlight, reminding Republicans that he governed the country's most populous state.

As Reagan's second term as governor came to an end in 1974, he decided not to seek a third term. In January 1975, he became a private citizen once again, but he was determined to stay in the public eye. He began writing a weekly

Elected president in 1968, Californian Richard Nixon helped governor Reagan by approving the state's requests for federal funds and projects.

newspaper column that was carried by many papers across the nation. He also taped news commentaries for broadcast on about 200 radio stations and made public appearances around the country.

Late in 1975, Ronald Reagan announced he would run for the Republican nomination for president even though the current president, Gerald Ford, was a

Republican and wanted to run for re-election. Ford had become vice president in 1973, then became president in August 1974 when President Richard Nixon resigned. He had been a longtime Republican leader in Congress and had broad support in the party.

Reagan stepped forward as the candidate of Republican conservatives. He believed that Ford was not anti-Communist enough in his foreign policy and that he did not fight big government strongly enough at home. Reagan spoke out against the Soviet Union and promised to slash federal spending, reduce taxes, and balance the budget. Reagan's positions appealed to his conservative followers, but Ford showed in the Republican primaries that he had much broader support. At the Republican convention that summer, Ford easily won the nomination.

The defeat was a low point for Reagan. He was 65 years old, and by the time of the next election he would be 69, older than any candidate ever elected to the presidency. When Ford lost the November election to Democrat Jimmy Carter, Republicans also blamed Reagan for dividing the party and reducing enthusiasm for Ford.

The next few years were quiet for Reagan. He continued writing his newspaper column and recording radio messages. He also studied politics and history. He was preparing for one last run for the highest office in the land.

Top, Reagan arrives at the 1976 Republican convention to challenge President Gerald Ford for the presidential nomination. Bottom, he confers with Ford after the president has won the nomination.

The Primary Campaign

When the Republican presidential primary contests started early in 1980, Reagan faced a field of lifelong politicians. George H. W. Bush had been a congressman, a diplomat, and the director of the Central Intelligence Agency. Robert Dole and Howard Baker had been influential Republican senators. Still, with his glamorous movie background and his eight years as governor, Reagan started out as the favorite. It appeared that George Bush would be his closest competitor.

Bush won the first test of strength in January, gaining the biggest following in the Iowa *caucuses* (a series of local meetings in which a party chooses its candidates). Reagan knew that he would have to do well in the next test, the New Hampshire primary. He campaigned long and hard there, traveling the state by bus. At one point, he made speeches on 21 consecutive days. On election day he won big, gaining 51 percent of the vote to Bush's 27 percent. This victory set Reagan on the path to the nomination. Of 33 primaries, he won 29 to Bush's 4.

At the Republican convention on July 16, 1980, Ronald Reagan received his party's nomination for president. He selected George Bush as his running mate. Bush was less conservative than Reagan, but he had a strong following in Texas and family ties to Republicans in the Northeast. In choosing Bush, Reagan reassured voters that his Republican administration would not be too conservative.

In 1980, Reagan won the Republican nomination for president on the first ballot. Later, he gave his acceptance speech to a wildly enthusiastic crowd.

In his acceptance speech, Reagan promised he would balance the budget, cut taxes, and reduce the size of government. At the end of his speech, he asked all in the convention hall to join him in a moment of prayer. Again and again through his political career, these were his favorite themes: lower taxes, smaller government, a balanced budget, and the power of religious faith.

The 1980 Campaign

Reagan ran against Democratic president Jimmy Carter, who had won the presidency four years earlier from Gerald Ford. Carter's term had been a discouraging period for the country. Inflation was eating away at the value of the dollar, and unemployment was high. Nearly a year before the election, radical Muslims in Iran had stormed the U.S. embassy in their capital, Tehran, and taken the U.S. embassy staff hostage. Carter tried to gain their release by diplomacy and by military action, but failed. As the election approached, his public approval rating had fallen below 20 percent.

Reagan relentlessly criticized Carter for both his foreign and domestic policies. Contrasting himself to Carter the negotiator, Reagan portrayed himself as a fighter, ready to stand up to America's enemies. He promised to make the country's military forces stronger. On the domestic front, Reagan said he had a plan to turn America's economy around. It involved deep cuts in taxes, reductions

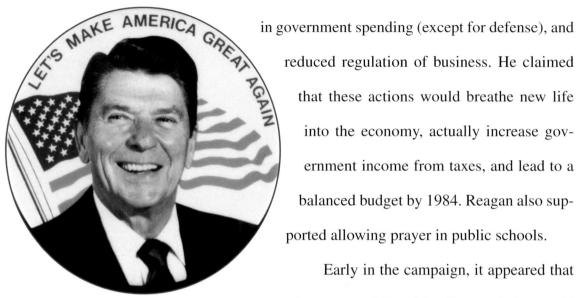

Reagan's campaign emphasized restoring Americans' confidence in themselves after years of doubt and dissension.

in government spending (except for defense), and reduced regulation of business. He claimed that these actions would breathe new life into the economy, actually increase government income from taxes, and lead to a balanced budget by 1984. Reagan also supported allowing prayer in public schools.

Early in the campaign, it appeared that the race would be tight. Carter tried to avoid a televised debate with Reagan, but the two rivals agreed to meet once, on October 28, only a week before the election. During the debate, Reagan appeared sharp and focused and ready for any question. Carter tried to rely on his experience as president, but still seemed indecisive. Finally, in his last chance to speak, Reagan summarized the choice for the voter. He said:

> Next Tuesday all of you will go to the polls, will stand there in the
>
> polling place and make a decision. I think when you make that
>
> decision, it might be well if you would ask yourself, are you better off
>
> than you were four years ago? Is it easier for you to go and buy things

in the stores than it was four years ago? Is there more or less

unemployment in the country than there was four years ago? Is

America as respected throughout the world as it was? Do you feel that

our security is as safe, that we're as strong as we were four years ago?

And if you answer all of those questions yes, why then, I think your

choice is very obvious. . . . If you don't agree . . . then I could suggest

another choice that you have.

Only days later, any chance Carter had to win re-election vanished when

negotiations for release of the hostages in Iran collapsed. Voters knew that the

hostages would not be coming home before the election. Even before the polls

closed on November 4, 1980, political experts were predicting a landslide victory

for the Reagan-Bush ticket. In fact, Reagan's victory was overwhelming. He

received 43.9 million votes to 35.5 million for Carter and 5.7 million for third-

party candidate John Anderson. In the Electoral College, Reagan won 44 states

with 489 electoral votes, while Carter won 6 states and the District of Columbia

with only 49 votes.

When Ronald Reagan took the oath of office on January 20, 1981, he

would be less than three weeks from his 70th birthday, the oldest man ever to take

on the presidency.

A Positive Note

From where he stood on his first inauguration day in the shadow of the U.S. Capitol, Ronald Reagan looked across a sea of faces westward toward the Washington Monument and the Lincoln Memorial. At his side, his wife Nancy watched with pride. His four children, Maureen, Michael, Patti, and Ron, were seated nearby.

He placed his hand on a Bible that had belonged to his mother and recited the oath of office. Then he launched into his inaugural address. His speech resonated with themes that had marked much of his life. He spoke of the importance of the individual and of the American dream. He also outlined a broad economic plan that included tax cuts and making government smaller by reining in spending. "It is time to . . . get government back within its means, and to lighten our punitive [punishing] tax burden," he said.

Reagan also promised Americans that their dreams and hopes and goals would be the dreams, hopes, and goals of his administration. "I believe we Americans are . . . ready to do what must be done to insure happiness and liberty for ourselves, our children, and our children's children." One woman who heard the president's speech said it reminded her of a Reagan movie with a happy ending. "Oh, it was so good it made me cry," she said.

Within hours after the inaugural speech, television broadcasters flashed live pictures of the American hostages in Iran being set free. Their release had been negotiated by President Jimmy Carter in the days before the inauguration, but the hostage-takers, who viewed Carter as an enemy, refused to let the hostages go until Ronald Reagan was president. The release of the hostages so soon after the inauguration suggested that America was already in better shape with Reagan as its leader.

One of Reagan's first jobs after the inauguration was to pick his cabinet and top aides. He chose Alexander Haig, a retired army general and a former aide to Richard Nixon, as secretary of state. As secretary of defense he chose Californian Caspar Weinberger, who had served as Reagan's budget director in California and later in President Nixon's cabinet. Reagan chose Edwin Meese III, his campaign manager, as counselor to the president with cabinet rank. Finally, Reagan called on James A. Baker III, George Bush's campaign manager during the primaries, to serve as White House chief of staff.

Only a week after Reagan took office, the hostages released by Iran arrived in Washington. They were greeted by crowds waving yellow ribbons and American flags.

The Reagan White House ————————————————

As he had done as governor, Reagan typically worked regular hours and paid attention to the "big picture." Unlike many earlier presidents, he delegated broad responsibilities to his staff and department heads and refused to involve himself in details. He nearly always got a good night's sleep and took a nap in the afternoon. In addition, he took frequent vacations at Camp David, the presidential retreat in Maryland, and at the Reagan ranch in California.

The Reagans brought a new kind of social life to the White House, too. Where Jimmy and Rosalynn Carter had lived simply, the Reagans liked entertaining and big parties. The new first couple renovated the White House family quarters, spending more than $800,000 raised by wealthy supporters, and they sponsored a regular round of parties—some for foreign dignitaries and some for their friends from California. Entertainment reporters called Washington "Hollywood on the Potomac."

An Assassin's Bullet ————————————————

On March 30, 1981, just nine weeks after taking office, Reagan was shot and seriously wounded outside a Washington hotel. Three other men were also wounded by the assassin. The president was rushed to George Washington University Hospital, where doctors found the bullet that had entered his lung and was lodged less than an inch from his heart. According to the surgeon who removed the bullet, President Reagan was "right on the margin" of death.

Despite the shock and the pain, the president kept his sense of humor. When he was introduced to the surgeons who would operate on him, he said, "Please tell me you're Republicans." When he saw Nancy Reagan after the shooting, he said, "Honey, I forgot to duck." The assassination attempt united the country as Republicans, Democrats, independents, and people who never voted united in their hope for the president's recovery.

Reagan made a quick recovery. Less than a month after the shooting he addressed Congress, urging the passage of his economic package. Of the others injured in the attack, two also recovered quickly. James Brady, Reagan's press secretary, was not so fortunate. Shot in the head, he was left with permanent brain damage.

At trial, the assassin, John Hinckley Jr., was found not guilty by reason of

President Reagan walks out of the hospital on April 11, 1981, twelve days after he was shot.

The Brady Bill

The attempted assassination and the grave injuries to Press Secretary James Brady brought about a movement to put restrictions on the sale of handguns. Twelve years later, in 1993, the Brady Bill was finally passed into law. It imposed a waiting period of five business days for the purchaser of a handgun while local police conducted a background check. The law was later changed, allowing the background check to be accomplished in minutes through use of a national computer system.

☆ ☆ ☆

Reagan's press secretary, James Brady, was permanently disabled during the assassination attempt, but he returned to the White House for a visit in November 1981.

insanity. He testified that he tried to kill the president to gain the approval of a popular young movie star named Jody Foster. He was sent to a psychiatric hospital near Washington, where he was still living under guard when Reagan died 23 years later.

The shooting left Reagan with a sense of his own mortality. He came to believe that he had survived the assassination attempt so that he could achieve something important in the years he had left.

Reaganomics

The central promise Reagan made as president was to reform government spending in the hope of improving the national economy. The plan he proposed, with the help of leading economists, came to be known as "Reaganomics." It had two parts. The first was to reduce the role of government in the economy by reducing government spending and easing regulation of business. The second was to reduce taxes, especially personal income taxes, which brought in most of the government's income.

Just two weeks after taking office, the new president delivered a major speech on his plan from the Oval Office. He began by saying the country was in the worst shape it had been in since the Great Depression, when about a quarter of America's workers were unemployed. In 1981 interest rates were soaring and economic growth was at a standstill. "It's time to try something different," Reagan said.

Since 1933, when President Franklin D. Roosevelt used government intervention to address the Great Depression, the federal government had spent vast amounts of money on broad new programs to address social ills. As it took on new responsibilities, the government grew. Now Reagan wanted to reverse that growth. He wanted to reduce the government's responsibilities and its size, ending some government programs and cutting back on many others. He made one huge exception—even while other costs were cut, he wanted large increases in expenditures for military defense.

At the same time, he wanted to slash taxes to the bone. Here, he and his advisers had a special wrinkle in their argument. They claimed that when the government reduced tax rates, the economy would boom and businesses would prosper. More people would have jobs and would earn more money. As a result, the government would soon be taking in even more tax dollars than before. This "supply-side" theory impressed many, but it struck others as too optimistic. When George Bush was running against Reagan for the Republican nomination, he called the theory "voodoo economics."

President Reagan signs the landmark bill reducing federal taxes and the federal budget in August 1981 at his ranch in California.

Riding a wave of good feeling following his recovery from the assassination attempt, Reagan was in a perfect position to push his "Reagan revolution" through Congress. In the summer of 1981, Congress approved cuts in government programs of $63 billion and an increase of $28 billion in defense spending, for an overall budget reduction of $35 billion. In addition, lawmakers passed the largest federal tax reductions up to that point in history.

Financial Trouble

Even with the budget cuts, the federal government's budget *deficit* (the amount by which the government's expenses in a year were greater than its income) kept increasing. Reagan's reduced tax rates and a sluggish economy kept the government's income from rising, while its expenses kept growing. In 1981, Reagan's first year in office, the federal government paid out $79 billion more than it took in. By 1983 the deficit had increased to $207 billion, by far the biggest deficit in U.S. history up to that time. Democrats in Congress and some economists urged the president to support a tax increase. At first he refused, but he finally agreed to increase certain taxes to bring in an additional $100 billion per year. Reagan refused to call the increases taxes, referring to them instead as "revenue enhancers." The increases helped bring the deficit down in 1984. The economy also began to pull out of its recession. Stock prices increased, and businesses began hiring new workers. During the rest of Reagan's years in the White House, economic growth was strong for the first time in a dozen years.

Reagan succeeded in passing his programs, but his opponents continued to criticize them. They pointed out that his budget cuts most seriously affected the nation's poorest and most helpless people. The government had tightened eligibility rules for unemployment payments, food stamps (used by the poor to buy food), and other welfare programs, ending these benefits for thousands. At the same time, critics said, Reagan's tax cuts were not helping the poor or the middle class very much, but mainly benefited the wealthy.

The War Against Communism

Reagan brought a major change to U.S. dealings with the *Soviet Union*, the Communist state that included present-day Russia and more than a dozen smaller republics. During the 1970s, presidents had been seeking ways to reduce tensions with the Soviets through negotiation and diplomacy. Reagan called the Soviet Union "the evil empire," and believed that the only way to negotiate with its leaders was from a position of superior strength. For this reason he insisted on large increases in military spending. In 1982 the United States faced growing world criticism because of its plans to position thousands of new missiles in Western Europe, aimed at Soviet cities.

In March 1983, the president went a step further. He proposed a visionary, long-term research project to develop a system that would shoot down enemy missiles before they reached their targets. He called it the Strategic Defense Initiative, or SDI. The details were so vague and unlikely that newspapers were soon calling the plan the "Star Wars" initiative, after the series of science fiction films that were then wildly popular.

The Soviet leadership reacted harshly to Reagan's strong language and to his actions. In November 1983, when the first new missiles arrived in Europe for deployment, the Soviets called off talks with the United States on arms reduction. It appeared to Reagan's critics that he was asking for a nuclear confrontation with the Soviets.

The president also favored taking strong steps against any socialist or Communist government in the world. In the Central American country of Nicaragua, a socialist party called the Sandinistas had overthrown a dictatorial government in 1979. Even though they liberalized Nicaragua, bringing education and new economic opportunities to the poor, Reagan considered them Communists. At his urging, the Central Intelligence Agency began to organize and train a "counterrevolutionary" force, known as the Contras, to attack the Nicaraguan government. In the rest of Central America, the Reagan administration supported governments that were anti-Communist but also dictatorial.

When the secret program to train and arm the Contras was revealed, members of Congress objected. They argued that President Reagan was interfering in the internal affairs of an independent country. In 1982 they passed an act forbidding any U.S. aid to antigovernment forces in Nicaragua, and in 1983 they passed an even stronger act. Their action and Reagan's reaction would lead to a major scandal in coming years.

Late in 1983, the president took action against an even smaller country than Nicaragua. A Communist government took over the tiny Caribbean island of Grenada, and soon afterward, laborers from Communist Cuba arrived in Grenada to help build an airport. Grenadians claimed the airport was intended to attract tourists to the island, but Reagan and his advisers feared that it might be used by Cubans and Soviets as a military base. It happened that several hundred Americans were studying at a medical school in Grenada. Expressing fears for their safety, the president sent 5,000 troops to occupy the defenseless island. The American occupiers turned the Grenadian government out of office and arranged for new elections to elect a non-Communist government. Then they withdrew. The brief and nearly bloodless "war" proved to be popular with many Americans.

Terror and the Middle East ———————

The administration's biggest setback in foreign policy occurred in the Middle Eastern country of Lebanon. The country was torn by strife between Muslim and Christian militias, which were seeking control of its government. The militias received support from the neighboring countries of Syria and Israel. After European nations sent peacekeeping troops to the country, Reagan agreed to send a contingent of U.S. Marines to contribute to the efforts. Muslim forces in Lebanon were soon unhappy that the U.S. forces favored the Christian militias. In April 1983, they sent a suicide bomber to attack the U.S. embassy in Beirut, Lebanon's capital, killing 63 people. Six months later, on October 23, another terrorist crashed a truck filled with explosives into a U.S. Marine barracks. The

President and Mrs. Reagan pay their respects to the marines who were killed in the bombing of the marine barracks in Beirut, Lebanon, in April 1983.

devastating explosion killed 241 American servicemen and women. On the same day, another terrorist bomb killed 58 French troops nearby.

"Nancy and I were in a state of grief, made almost speechless by the magnitude of the loss," Reagan later said. He continued to defend the U.S. role in Lebanon, but early in 1984 he withdrew the marines.

Other Victories

In the summer of 1984, the president had a chance to recall one of the great victories in U.S. history. He traveled to the beaches of Normandy in France to celebrate the 40th anniversary of D-Day, June 6, 1944, when Allied forces landed in German-occupied France. At Pointe du Hoc, the scene of some of the fiercest fighting, Reagan delivered one of his most memorable speeches. The trip marked a high point in his presidency.

Chapter 5

"Morning in America" —————————

Despite setbacks and tragedies, President Reagan remained popular with many Americans. As 1984 dawned, the long recession seemed to be over, reinforcing the president's sunny optimism. His skills as a communicator enabled him to sell his ideas even to many Democrats. There was no doubt that he would be nominated by his party to seek a second term as president.

At the Republican convention in Dallas in August, Ronald Reagan accepted his party's nomination with a rousing speech that was interrupted dozens of times by an enthusiastic audience chanting, "Four more years!" and "U-S-A!" During the campaign, millions saw a Reagan advertisement with a simple theme: "It's morning again in America." The ad pointed out the improvement in the country's economy and in its mood, and it concluded, "Why would we want to return to where we were, less than four short years ago?"

Reagan and Vice President Bush were nominated for re-election at the 1984 Republican convention.

The Democrats nominated Walter Mondale, vice president under Jimmy

Carter from 1977 to 1981, and a longtime senator from Minnesota. Mondale

made history when he selected Geraldine Ferraro as his vice-presidential running

mate. She became the first woman ever nominated for vice president by a major

The New Right

Reagan's victories in two presidential elections helped bring success to a coalition known as the "New Right." This movement, which got its start in the 1964 campaign of Barry Goldwater, was a crusade against the "liberal" politics of the Democratic party. The New Right wanted to reduce the size and reach of government, advocating lower taxes and less government regulation of business. At the same time, it favored "family values," which it defined as support for traditional families and opposition to abortion rights, and it supported "law and order," including strong enforcement of drug laws. Many in the New Right were evangelical Christians and belonged to such groups as the Moral Majority, formed by evangelist Jerry Falwell in the early 1980s.

☆ ☆ ☆

party. Ferraro was serving her third term in the U.S. House of Representatives from a district in New York City. From the beginning, the Mondale-Ferraro ticket had an uphill battle. Mondale never found a message that was as positive and inspiring as Reagan's, and he could not deny that times were good economically. Instead, he charged that during a second term the president would reduce Social Security payments to retired Americans and that Reagan deficits might send the country into bankruptcy.

At one point, Mondale suggested he was more honest than Reagan. He asserted that Reagan would have to raise taxes to reduce the deficit. "I will raise

Vice President Bush greets Democratic vice-presidential candidate Geraldine Ferraro before their televised debate. Ms. Ferraro was the first woman nominated for vice president by a major party.

your taxes, too," he continued. "The difference is that he doesn't want to tell you, and I just did." The Democratic hopeful learned that honesty is not always the best policy. American voters did not want to hear that anyone might raise their taxes.

Democratic hopes for victory ultimately hinged on the two televised debates between Reagan and Mondale. In the first debate, the president seemed confused, lost, and unsure of himself. His supporters were shocked, and Democrats were overjoyed. The president himself had raised the issue of his age. If he was re-elected, he would turn 74 a few weeks after his inauguration. He was already the oldest person ever to serve as president. Was he still up to the job?

In the second debate, however, Reagan turned the tables. Mondale, worn out by weeks of strenuous campaigning, looked old and tired. Reagan radiated confidence. When one of the newsmen asked about his age, Reagan replied, "I will not make age an issue of this campaign. I am not going to exploit, for political purposes, my opponent's youth and inexperience." Even the 56-year-old Mondale had to laugh. As he had often done in the past, Reagan had used humor to deflect an opponent's point. He had buried the age issue once and for all.

Reagan's optimism carried him back into the White House on a huge wave of popularity. The Reagan-Bush ticket won 59 percent of the popular vote and captured 49 states with 525 electoral votes. Mondale won his home state of Minnesota and the District of Columbia with only 13 electoral votes. The only

President Reagan campaigns for re-election at a youth rally. Even though he was the oldest person to serve as president, he had strong support from young voters.

troubling issue for Republicans was that their congressional candidates were not nearly as popular as their president. Democrats continued to hold a substantial majority in the House of Representatives, and Republicans had only a 53–47 majority in the Senate.

Domestic Issues

In mid-1985, doctors discovered small growths in President Reagan's large intestine. He entered the hospital on July 12 to have them removed. Surgeons found that the growths were malignant (cancerous), so the operation was extended to remove all the cancerous tissue. Despite his age, Reagan proved to be in good physical condition, and he recovered quickly. He returned to the White House only a week after the surgery.

During 1985 Reagan and his advisers worked with Congress on a new bill to reform and simplify the tax code. Since high deficits still threatened, Reagan had given up hopes for another tax cut, but he believed that the government could increase its income without raising taxes by closing loopholes in tax laws that allowed taxpayers to avoid paying their full share. The bill finally passed in 1986. In the next two years, the booming economy helped keep the budget deficit down.

In January 1986, the United States prepared to launch the space shuttle *Challenger* into space. Since the early 1980s, the program had successfully launched two dozen manned space shuttles. The mission in early 1986 was special. For the first time, a nonastronaut was part of the shuttle crew. She was Christa McAuliffe, a teacher from Concord, New Hampshire. Around the country, millions of schoolchildren gathered around television sets to watch the shuttle lift off. Just over a minute after leaving the launchpad, *Challenger* exploded in a ball of fire and smoke. All six members of the crew were killed. The incident devastated the students and parents who were watching. At a memorial for the crew, President Reagan gave a touching speech that helped the nation deal with its grief.

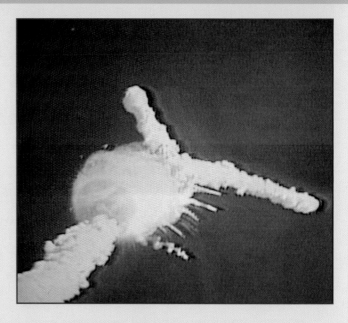

The space shuttle *Challenger* explodes seconds after lifting off from Cape Kennedy on January 28, 1986. All seven crew members, including schoolteacher Christa McAuliffe, were killed. President Reagan led the nation in grieving for the tragedy.

☆ ☆ ☆

Foreign Policy

The great turnaround in Reagan's presidency came in his policies toward the Soviet Union. During his first term, his outspoken statements and U.S. actions challenged the Soviets and increased tensions between the two nations. Reagan's opponents feared that his actions might lead to a nuclear war.

Even before his first term ended, however, Reagan's position seemed to soften. Early in 1984, in his state of the union address to Congress, he expressed the hope that discussions about arms reductions could be started again. In 1985, he announced an agreement to meet with the Soviet leader Konstantin Chernenko for talks in Geneva, Switzerland. Chernenko died before the meetings took place, however. Instead, Reagan met the new Soviet leader, a younger man named Mikhail Gorbachev. At their meeting, the two men struck up a friendship. Gorbachev was determined to bring important reforms to the Soviet government and economy. Reagan liked the new leader and felt that he could trust him. They discussed the need to reduce the buildup of nuclear arms.

After further negotiations by others, Reagan and Gorbachev met again in Reykjavik, Iceland, in October 1986. This time they discussed a sweeping agreement to reduce nuclear arms. The plan called for the elimination of intermediate-range missiles and a major reduction of long-range missiles. It appeared that this quiet meeting between world leaders might lead to a far-reaching agreement, but

President Reagan and Soviet premier Mikhail Gorbachev meet in Reykjavik, Iceland, in 1986. Reagan was a stern foe of the Soviet Union, but he formed a warm friendship with Mr. Gorbachev.

there was one obstacle. Gorbachev insisted that the United States agree not to deploy its "Star Wars" missile defense system. Even though the system would not be ready for at least ten years, Reagan refused to make any such agreement. The summit ended on an awkward note.

The story did have a happy ending, however. American and Soviet negotiators continued to meet, and finally, in December 1987, Gorbachev visited Washington, where the two leaders signed the Treaty on the Elimination of Intermediate-Range and Shorter Range Nuclear Forces (known as INF). The U.S. Senate ratified the treaty in May 1988.

Iran-Contra

Just as President Reagan was preparing to fly to Iceland to meet Gorbachev in October 1986, an ugly scandal began when a U.S. plane was shot down by troops of the Nicaraguan government. The scandal, which came to be known as "Iran-Contra," would taint the president and many of his closest advisers.

In 1982 and 1983, Congress had passed laws clearly forbidding the U.S. government to provide military support to the Contras, who were trying to overthrow the socialist government of Nicaragua. When Nicaraguan government troops shot down the U.S. plane in October 1986, however, they discovered that it was loaded with weapons and ammunition. A surviving U.S. crew member confessed that the cargo was intended for the Contra fighters. Clearly someone in the U.S. government was continuing to supply the Contras and directly disobeying the law.

Early in November 1986, another scandal appeared. A Middle Eastern newspaper reported that a U.S. hostage in the Middle East had been released in return for U.S. arms shipments to Iran. Soon the story was appearing in major U.S. newspapers. Iran was still an enemy of the United States, and government policy strictly prohibited paying any kind of ransom for hostages. Who in the U.S. government would agree to such a deal?

Finally, late in November, the two scandals were brought together. It was revealed that the United States had sold some weapons to Iran for cash and used the money to buy arms and ammunition for the Contras in Nicaragua. On November 25, Reagan's national security adviser, John M. Poindexter, and a national security aide, Oliver North, resigned because of their involvement in the complicated plot. The president denied any involvement, but his approval rating dropped from 61 percent to 47 percent in a single month.

As the matter was investigated by a congressional committee and a special prosecutor, it became clear that the public did not believe the president's claims of innocence. There were calls from Democrats in Congress for impeachment proceedings against him. Finally, on March 4, 1987, the president made a nationally televised address. In it he said:

A few months ago I told the American people I did not trade arms for hostages. My heart and my best intentions tell me that's true, but the facts and evidence tell me it is not. As [investigations] reported, what began as a strategic opening to Iran deteriorated, in its implementation, into trading arms for hostages. This runs counter to my own beliefs, to administration policy, and to the original strategy we had in mind.

There are reasons why it happened, but no excuses. It was a mistake.

Reagan's fans saw the speech as an acceptance of responsibility, while his critics accused him of evading the issue. In any case, his approval ratings rose once again, and the threat of impeachment began to recede. Poindexter, North, and others were convicted of crimes in the Iran-Contra scandal, but in nearly every case, the convictions were overturned on technicalities. Late in 1992, President George Bush (who had been a target of Iran-Contra accusations for his actions as vice president) pardoned the remaining figures in the scandal.

Iran-Contra cast a shadow over Reagan's second term, but his personal popularity survived. Once again he lived up to a nickname invented by Democratic representative Patricia Schroeder. She dubbed Reagan "the Teflon president." Just as no food sticks to a Teflon skillet, no scandal seemed to stick to Reagan's reputation.

The Decline of Communism

In June 1987, President Reagan visited Berlin, the city that was divided by a wall separating the East from the West. The wall was built by Communist East Germany to keep its own people from escaping to the democratic West. Reagan spoke to a large crowd from a stand in front of the historic Brandenburg Gate, which was a part of the East-West border. In a ringing challenge to Communism in Eastern Europe, the president addressed his friend and negotiating partner, Mikhail Gorbachev:

> General Secretary Gorbachev, if you seek peace, if you seek prosperity
> for the Soviet Union and Eastern Europe, if you seek liberalization:
> Come here to this gate! Mr. Gorbachev, open this gate! Mr. Gorbachev,
> tear down this wall!

Neither Gorbachev nor the East German authorities immediately tore down that wall, but the stern rule of Soviet Communism in Eastern Europe was loosening with each passing day. In November 1989, two and a half years after Reagan's speech, East Germany announced the end of all travel restrictions, and within months, the hated Berlin Wall was torn down. Communist rule in the Soviet Union was also beginning to loosen, as Premier Gorbachev introduced

Reagan speaks in West Berlin in June 1987. Behind him is the Brandenburg Gate, which served as part of the wall separating East and West Berlin. Reagan urged his friend Mikhail Gorbachev to "tear down this wall!"

political and economic reforms. Late in 1991, Gorbachev formally dissolved the Soviet Union, leaving its 15 separate republics to become independent countries.

Wall Street Jitters

In the United States, 1987 was a boom year. That fall, the stock market reached all-time highs. Unemployment was low, and signs seemed to point to continued good times. Then, in mid-October, the stock market took a dive. It began to fall on Friday, October 16, but no one was prepared for the events of Monday, October 19. The Dow Jones Industrial Average fell 508 points, from 2,246 to 1,738, losing 22.6 percent of its value. It was the greatest single-day decline ever seen.

The sudden crash resulted in huge changes on Wall Street, the center of stock trading in New York. More than 15,000 workers in the financial industry lost their jobs as companies struggled to make up for their losses. There were fears that the crash might signal the beginning of a new recession. Fortunately, the market recovered fairly quickly, and there were no signs of a new recession.

The Reagan Revolution Continues

Early in 1988, Republicans began making preparations for the November presidential election. Vice President George Bush announced his candidacy for the

Panicky stock traders try to sell their holdings on the New York Stock Exchange on October 19, 1987. Prices fell more than 500 points in a single day.

President Reagan and Vice President Bush receive applause from the president's cabinet after Reagan has endorsed Bush for president in 1988.

nomination, and President Reagan endorsed him. Despite the ups and downs of his administration, Reagan's popularity remained high. Near the end of his term he was still viewed favorably by 63 percent of all Americans.

At the Republican convention in New Orleans, Bush pledged to continue the policies of the Reagan administration. In November he was elected, defeating Democratic candidate Michael Dukakis.

Return to California ——————————

On January 20, 1989, Ronald Reagan and his wife, Nancy, climbed aboard a helicopter on the White House lawn. As the craft slowly circled, they took a last look at the house that had been their home for eight years. Now they were leaving to begin a new life.

Soon the Reagans were flying west across the country. In what seemed the blink of an eye, Washington and the pomp and circumstance of the presidency were behind them, and they were back in California.

After years in the limelight, at the center of world affairs, Reagan was retired at the age of 78. While he was no longer a star on the world's stage, Reagan was far from idle. Almost immediately, he set out to write his autobiography, *An American Life*, which became a best seller. Reagan, always an accomplished horseman, relaxed by riding on his ranch and by chopping firewood.

President Reagan on his beloved ranch near Santa Barbara, California.

Not long after leaving the White House, the Reagans received a new home in the fashionable Bel Air section of Los Angeles, near Hollywood, paid for by contributions from their longtime supporters. There the Reagans were able to relax in comfort. They regularly attended the nearby Bel Air Presbyterian Church.

Reagan, the man who years earlier was paid to speak on behalf of General Electric and who gained fame as the "Great Communicator," also became a paid speaker. Not long after leaving the White House, he was paid roughly $2 million, much more than he made for his entire service as president, to make two 20-minute speeches to a group of businessmen in Japan.

Fading from Sight

During Reagan's second term in the White House rumors abounded that his mental abilities were impaired. Insiders reported that he had a difficult time concentrating and suffered from memory lapses. Reagan himself used to joke that he was becoming forgetful.

By 1993, four years after he left the presidency, Reagan's memory lapses were becoming serious. Doctors who examined him late that year detected signs of Alzheimer's disease, which gradually causes memory loss and other mental changes. In the late stages of the disease, a patient requires constant care.

Nancy Reagan

Throughout Reagan's political career and into his last years, his wife Nancy was his constant companion and most faithful supporter. The daughter of an actress and adopted daughter of a neurosurgeon, she was born Anne Frances Robbins in New York City on July 6, 1921. She graduated from Smith College, where she studied drama, then came to Hollywood. She was known as Nancy Davis, using her longtime nickname and the last name of her adoptive father.

Nancy Reagan later said that her life really began with her marriage to Reagan in 1952. She took an active interest in his political career. During his time in the White House, Nancy Reagan championed the "Just Say No" campaign against illegal drug use, which emphasized old-fashioned willpower to overcome temptation.

Nancy Reagan also became a powerful force in politics. She was fiercely protective of the president and helped determine his schedule. White House staff members who crossed her sometimes found themselves unable to meet with the president. Her critics accused her of spending lavishly for clothes and other personal items, and mocked her for relying on astrology in making important decisions.

In the Reagans' retirement years, Nancy became something of a heroine when she personally cared for the president through his long last illness.

☆ ★ ☆

On November 5, 1994, Reagan released a letter in his own handwriting, announcing his illness. It sounded the same optimistic notes Reagan had used throughout his life, but it also looked honestly at what the future would hold for him and his family. In part, this is what it said:

At the moment I feel just fine. I intend to live the remainder of the years God gives me on this earth doing the things I have always done. I will continue to share life's journey with my beloved Nancy and my family. I plan to enjoy the great outdoors and stay in touch with my friends and supporters.

Unfortunately, as Alzheimer's disease progresses, the family often bears a heavy burden. I only wish there was some way I could spare Nancy from this painful experience. When the time comes I am confident that with your help she will face it with faith and courage. . . .

I now begin the journey that will lead me into the sunset of my life. I know that for America there will always be a bright dawn ahead.

The End of the Road

Following this public announcement of his illness, the former president retreated from public view. He remained at his home in California, where he was cared for by his wife, Nancy, as his memory slipped away. In 2001, Reagan, then 90 years old, slipped and fell, breaking his hip. From that point on, he was confined to bed. His health steadily worsened.

During these years, Reagan's many fans took steps to memorialize his life and presidency. In 1998 Washington National Airport was renamed the Ronald Reagan Washington National Airport. In 2001 the U.S. Navy christened an aircraft carrier the USS *Ronald Reagan*. Very few navy ships in history have been named for living individuals. Many other federal buildings throughout the country have been named in honor of Reagan. In addition, there are some supporters of Reagan who hope to have his face shown on the ten, twenty, or fifty dollar bill.

Nearly ten years after announcing his illness, Ronald Reagan died at his home in Bel Air, California, on June 5, 2004. When he died, his wife Nancy and their two children, Patti and Ron, were with him. Reagan's adopted son Michael arrived soon afterward. His oldest daughter, Maureen, had died in 2001.

The former president received a full state funeral in Washington, D.C., on June 11. It was the first state funeral since the death of former president Lyndon Johnson in 1973. Some 4,000 people attended the service at the National Cathedral. Those attending included President George W. Bush; former presidents Ford, Carter, Clinton, and George H. W. Bush; former Soviet leader Mikhail Gorbachev; and former British prime minister Margaret Thatcher. Later that same day, Reagan was buried in a private ceremony at the Ronald Reagan Presidential Library in California.

President Reagan's casket is carried out of the church after funeral services on June 11, 2004. Mrs. Reagan is at the left. Beyond the coffin are President George W. Bush and former presidents Bush, Carter, Ford, and Clinton, and their wives.

The Reagan Revolution

Ronald Reagan's presidency marked an important turning point in American history. He was elected on his pledges to reduce the reach and the costs of the federal government. During his eight years in office, Reagan helped change the direction of government, beginning the "Reagan Revolution." The conservative values he favored helped elect George H. W. Bush in 1988 and George W. Bush in 2000 and 2004. The revolution affected Democrats as well as Republicans. President Bill Clinton, who was elected president in 1992 and 1996, agreed with Reagan that "government is not the answer" to every social or economic problem. Reagan and his successors succeeded in making "liberal" a term of abuse.

Reagan's revolution was held back by his inconsistent policies in economics. He succeeded in granting large tax cuts both to individuals and to businesses. He was much less successful in reducing federal spending, mainly because he favored large increases in military spending and because he refused to limit the growth of Social Security payments, which provide retirement income for millions of Americans. As a result, the Reagan administration brought about some of the largest deficits in U.S. history. His critics claim that these deficits endangered the economic health of the country.

Ronald Reagan.

The Fall of Communism ———————————

Ronald Reagan may be longest remembered for another revolution in world affairs. During his eight years in office, the powerful Soviet Union came to the edge of collapse, ending years of tense Cold War competition between the United States and the Soviets. Conservative supporters of Reagan claim that he played a major role in bringing down the Soviet empire by increasing defense spending and beginning development of the "Star Wars" defense plan to intercept nuclear missiles. These challenges may have caused Soviet leaders to give up their arms race with the West.

Other observers point out that Reagan began as an enemy of the Soviet Union, but that he befriended Mikhail Gorbachev, encouraged peaceful change in the Soviet Union, and negotiated the landmark INF treaty, greatly reducing nuclear armaments. These observers suggest that Reagan accomplished more as a peacemaker than as a warlike adversary.

However it was accomplished, the downfall of the Soviet Union and its Communist satellite states occurred soon after Reagan left office. This major turning point in world affairs will always be associated with Reagan and his administration.

The Great Communicator

Finally, Reagan will be remembered as one of the country's most popular and beloved presidents. He was able to communicate with average citizens in a way few president have ever managed. He was able to convince friends and opponents alike to see his point of view and often to follow where he led. He was not so well versed in the fine points of politics and government as other presidents, but he ran an effective presidential administration. He made use of experts and delegated authority to others. In the meantime, he kept his eye on the big picture. Americans found his style down-to-earth and reassuring.

The president had blind spots, too. He and his conservative philosophy seemed to have little sympathy for the poor, for minorities, or for those afflicted by drug addiction or sexually transmitted diseases. He and his supporters seemed to suggest that the poor and afflicted could solve their own problems with willpower and determination—and without the help of government.

When asked himself how he thought history would remember him, Reagan mentioned the country's morale. He said, "I hope it will remember . . . that I wanted to see if the American people couldn't get back that pride, and that patriotism, that confidence that they had in our system. And I think they have."

Fast Facts Ronald Wilson Reagan

Birth:	February 6, 1911
Birthplace:	Tampico, Illinois
Parents:	John Reagan and Nelle Wilson Reagan
Brother:	Neil Reagan (1908–1996)
Education:	Eureka College, Eureka, Illinois, graduated 1932
Occupations:	Radio announcer, actor, political leader
Marriages:	To Jane Wyman, January 24, 1940 (divorced 1949)
	To Nancy Davis, March 4, 1952
Children:	With Jane Wyman:
	Maureen (1941–2001)
	Michael (1945–)
	With Nancy Davis Reagan:
	Patti (1952–)
	Ronald (1958–)
Political Parties:	Democratic (to 1962); Republican
Public Offices:	1967–1975 Governor of California
	1981–1989 President of the United States
His Vice President:	George Herbert Walker Bush
Major Actions as President:	1981 Welcomed freed hostages from Iran
	1981 Survived assassination attempt
	1981 Signed bills cutting budget and taxes
	1983 Sent U.S. forces to Lebanon
	1983 Sent U.S. military forces to occupy Grenada
	1987 Admitted involvement in Iran-Contra affair
	1987 Signed INF treaty reducing nuclear armaments
Death:	Bel Air, California, June 5, 2004
Age at Death:	93 years
Burial Place:	Ronald Reagan Presidential Library, California

Fast Facts Nancy Davis Reagan

Birth:	Born Anne Frances Robbins, July 6, 1921
Birthplace:	New York City
Parents:	Kenneth and Edith Robbins
	Adopted by stepfather Loyal Davis, 1928, took his last name
Education:	Smith College, graduated 1943
Marriage:	To Ronald Wilson Reagan, March 4, 1952
Children:	Patti (1952–)
	Ronald (1958–)
Stepchildren:	Maureen (1941–2001)
	Michael (1945–)

Timeline

1911	1920	1928	1932	1934
Ronald Wilson Reagan is born in Tampico, Illinois, February 6.	Family moves to Dixon, Illinois.	Reagan graduates from Dixon Northside High School.	Graduates from Eureka College.	Becomes radio sports announcer in Des Moines, Iowa.

1947	1949	1952	1954	1958
Elected president of the Screen Actors Guild, serves to 1952.	Reagan and Jane Wyman divorce.	Reagan marries actress Nancy Davis; daughter Patti is born.	Reagan becomes host of weekly television show, *General Electric Theater*.	Son Ronald Jr. is born.

1981	1983	1984	1986	1987
Survives assassination attempt, March; signs budget and tax cut bills.	241 U.S. Marines killed in terrorist attack in Lebanon; U.S. attacks Caribbean island of Grenada.	Reagan wins election to second term.	Space shuttle *Challenger* explodes; Iran-Contra scandal disclosed.	Reagan signs INF treaty with Soviet leader Mikhail Gorbachev, reducing nuclear armaments.

1937

Gets first acting contract in Hollywood, appears in first movie.

1940

Appears in *Knute Rockne—All American*; marries actress Jane Wyman.

1941

Daughter Maureen born; U.S. enters World War II after attack on Pearl Harbor.

1942

Reagan joins armed forces, serves to 1945.

1945

Resumes his acting career; Reagans adopt son Michael.

1962

Reagan joins the Republican party.

1964

Campaigns for Republican presidential candidate Barry Goldwater.

1966

Elected governor of California, serves until 1975.

1976

Makes losing effort to gain Republican presidential nomination.

1980

Chosen Republican presidential candidate, August; elected president, November.

1988

Vice President George H. W. Bush elected president.

1989

Reagan retires to California.

1994

Announces he is suffering from Alzheimer's disease.

2004

Dies June 5.

Glossary

★ ★ ★ ★ ★

blacklist: a list kept by an employer of people it will not hire because they are considered unreliable or disreputable; in the 1950s movie studios kept a blacklist of workers suspected of Communist associations

caucus: a local meeting of a political group to discuss strategy or to endorse candidates for office

Communist: a member of a Communist party, or a believer in the Communist doctrine of state ownership of property and business

deficit: the amount by which a country's expenses in a year are greater than its income

endorse: to recommend officially; political organizations often endorse candidates for election

favorite son: a person whose name is placed in nomination at a political gathering by delegates from his own state or region as a sign of respect and admiration

Soviet Union: from 1921 to 1991, a country occupying northeastern Europe and northern Asia, consisting of present-day Russia and 15 smaller republics (now independent countries); the Soviet Union was the leading Communist country in the world and the major adversary of the United States from 1945 to 1991

union: an organization of workers which represents them in negotiations with management about pay and working conditions

Further Reading

Feinstein, Stephen. *The 1980s from Ronald Reagan to MTV*. Berkeley Heights, NJ: Enslow Publishers, 2000.

Klingel, Cynthia Fitterer, and Robert Noyed. *Ronald W. Reagan: Our Fortieth President*. Chanhassen, MN: Child's World, 2002.

Williams, Jean Kinney. *Ronald W. Reagan*. Minneapolis: Compass Point Books, 2003.

MORE ADVANCED READING

Cannon, Lou. *President Reagan: The Role of a Lifetime*. New York: Public Affairs, 2000.

D'Souza, Dinesh. *Ronald Reagan: How an Ordinary Man Became an Extraordinary Leader*. New York: Free Press, 1997.

Johnson, Haynes. *Sleepwalking through History: America in the Reagan Years*. New York: W.W. Norton, 2003.

Morris, Edmund. *Dutch: A Memoir of Ronald Reagan*. New York: Random House, 1999.

Places to Visit

★ ★ ★ ★ ★ ★

**Ronald Reagan Presidential Library
  and Museum**
40 Presidential Drive
P.O. Box 5020
Simi Valley, CA 93065
(805) 577-4000
http://www.reagan.utexas.edu

The museum portrays the life, leadership, and legacy of President Reagan. Exhibits include presidential papers and memorabilia. Ronald Reagan was buried near the library in 2004. The grave is visited by thousands of people each month.

California State Capitol
10th and L Streets
Sacramento, CA 95814
Tour office: (916) 324-0333
http://www.capitolmuseum.ca.gov/

Reagan served as governor here from 1967 to 1975.

The White House
1600 Pennsylvania Avenue NW
Washington, DC 20500
Visitors' Info: (202) 456-7041
http://www.whitehouse.gov/history/life/

Ronald and Nancy Reagan lived here from 1981 until 1989.

Online Sites of Interest

★ **Internet Public Library, Presidents of the United States (IPL POTUS)**

http:// www.potus.com/rwreagan.html

Includes concise information about Reagan and his presidency and provides links to other sites of interest.

★ **American President.org**

http://www.americanpresident.org/history/ronaldreagan/

Offers a biography of Ronald Reagan. This site also provides information on the presidency and biographies of all the presidents. It is maintained by the Miller Center of Public Affairs at the University of Virginia.

★ **Grolier**

http://gi.grolier.com/presidents/

This site, sponsored by the publisher of reference material, offers a selection of links leading to information about all the presidents. Material available includes presidential portraits and presidential election results.

★ **The White House**

www.whitehouse.gov/history/presidents

Offers brief biographical articles on each president and first lady.

Table of Presidents

	1. George Washington	2. John Adams	3. Thomas Jefferson	4. James Madison
Took office	Apr 30 1789	Mar 4 1797	Mar 4 1801	Mar 4 1809
Left office	Mar 3 1797	Mar 3 1801	Mar 3 1809	Mar 3 1817
Birthplace	Westmoreland Co, VA	Braintree, MA	Shadwell, VA	Port Conway, VA
Birth date	Feb 22 1732	Oct 20 1735	Apr 13 1743	Mar 16 1751
Death date	Dec 14 1799	July 4 1826	July 4 1826	June 28 1836

	9. William H. Harrison	10. John Tyler	11. James K. Polk	12. Zachary Taylor
Took office	Mar 4 1841	Apr 6 1841	Mar 4 1845	Mar 5 1849
Left office	**Apr 4 1841•**	Mar 3 1845	Mar 3 1849	**July 9 1850•**
Birthplace	Berkeley, VA	Greenway, VA	Mecklenburg Co, NC	Barboursville, VA
Birth date	Feb 9 1773	Mar 29 1790	Nov 2 1795	Nov 24 1784
Death date	Apr 4 1841	Jan 18 1862	June 15 1849	July 9 1850

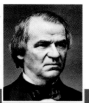   

	17. Andrew Johnson	18. Ulysses S. Grant	19. Rutherford B. Hayes	20. James A. Garfield
Took office	Apr 15 1865	Mar 4 1869	Mar 5 1877	Mar 4 1881
Left office	Mar 3 1869	Mar 3 1877	Mar 3 1881	**Sept 19 1881•**
Birthplace	Raleigh, NC	Point Pleasant, OH	Delaware, OH	Orange, OH
Birth date	Dec 29 1808	Apr 27 1822	Oct 4 1822	Nov 19 1831
Death date	July 31 1875	July 23 1885	Jan 17 1893	Sept 19 1881

5. James Monroe

Mar 4 1817

Mar 3 1825

Westmoreland Co, VA

Apr 28 1758

July 4 1831

6. John Quincy Adams

Mar 4 1825

Mar 3 1829

Braintree, MA

July 11 1767

Feb 23 1848

7. Andrew Jackson

Mar 4 1829

Mar 3 1837

The Waxhaws, SC

Mar 15 1767

June 8 1845

8. Martin Van Buren

Mar 4 1837

Mar 3 1841

Kinderhook, NY

Dec 5 1782

July 24 1862

13. Millard Fillmore

July 9 1850

Mar 3 1853

Locke Township, NY

Jan 7 1800

Mar 8 1874

14. Franklin Pierce

Mar 4 1853

Mar 3 1857

Hillsborough, NH

Nov 23 1804

Oct 8 1869

15. James Buchanan

Mar 4 1857

Mar 3 1861

Cove Gap, PA

Apr 23 1791

June 1 1868

16. Abraham Lincoln

Mar 4 1861

Apr 15 1865•

Hardin Co, KY

Feb 12 1809

Apr 15 1865

21. Chester A. Arthur

Sept 19 1881

Mar 3 1885

Fairfield, VT

Oct 5 1829

Nov 18 1886

22. Grover Cleveland

Mar 4 1885

Mar 3 1889

Caldwell, NJ

Mar 18 1837

June 24 1908

23. Benjamin Harrison

Mar 4 1889

Mar 3 1893

North Bend, OH

Aug 20 1833

Mar 13 1901

24. Grover Cleveland

Mar 4 1893

Mar 3 1897

Caldwell, NJ

Mar 18 1837

June 24 1908

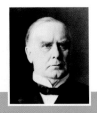

	25. William McKinley	**26. Theodore Roosevelt**	**27. William H. Taft**	**28. Woodrow Wilson**
Took office	Mar 4 1897	Sept 14 1901	Mar 4 1909	Mar 4 1913
Left office	**Sept 14 1901•**	Mar 3 1909	Mar 3 1913	Mar 3 1921
Birthplace	Niles, OH	New York, NY	Cincinnati, OH	Staunton, VA
Birth date	Jan 29 1843	Oct 27 1858	Sept 15 1857	Dec 28 1856
Death date	Sept 14 1901	Jan 6 1919	Mar 8 1930	Feb 3 1924

	33. Harry S. Truman	**34. Dwight D. Eisenhower**	**35. John F. Kennedy**	**36. Lyndon B. Johnson**
Took office	Apr 12 1945	Jan 20 1953	Jan 20 1961	Nov 22 1963
Left office	Jan 20 1953	Jan 20 1961	**Nov 22 1963•**	Jan 20 1969
Birthplace	Lamar, MO	Denison, TX	Brookline, MA	Johnson City, TX
Birth date	May 8 1884	Oct 14 1890	May 29 1917	Aug 27 1908
Death date	Dec 26 1972	Mar 28 1969	Nov 22 1963	Jan 22 1973

	41. George Bush	**42. Bill Clinton**	**43. George W. Bush**
Took office	Jan 20 1989	Jan 20 1993	Jan 20 2001
Left office	Jan 20 1993	Jan 20 2001	—
Birthplace	Milton, MA	Hope, AR	New Haven, CT
Birth date	June 12 1924	Aug 19 1946	July 6 1946
Death date	—	—	—

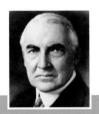

29. Warren G. Harding

Mar 4 1921

Aug 2 1923•

Blooming Grove, OH

Nov 21 1865

Aug 2 1923

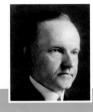

30. Calvin Coolidge

Aug 2 1923

Mar 3 1929

Plymouth, VT

July 4 1872

Jan 5 1933

31. Herbert Hoover

Mar 4 1929

Mar 3 1933

West Branch, IA

Aug 10 1874

Oct 20 1964

32. Franklin D. Roosevelt

Mar 4 1933

Apr 12 1945•

Hyde Park, NY

Jan 30 1882

Apr 12 1945

37. Richard M. Nixon

Jan 20 1969

Aug 9 1974★

Yorba Linda, CA

Jan 9 1913

Apr 22 1994

38. Gerald R. Ford

Aug 9 1974

Jan 20 1977

Omaha, NE

July 14 1913

—

39. Jimmy Carter

Jan 20 1977

Jan 20 1981

Plains, GA

Oct 1 1924

—

40. Ronald Reagan

Jan 20 1981

Jan 20 1989

Tampico, IL

Feb 6 1911

June 5 2004

• Indicates the president died while in office.

★ Richard Nixon resigned before his term expired.

Index

Page numbers in *italics* indicate illustrations.

Alzheimer's disease, 87
An American Life, 85
Anderson, John, 49
arms reductions, 73, 75
assassination attempt, 7, 9, 54–56

Baker, Howard, 45
Baker, James A., III, 52
Bedtime for Bonzo, 22
Berlin, Germany, 78, *79*, 80
Berlin Wall, 78, *79*
Birch Society. *See* John Birch Society
blacklist, 27
Brady, James, 55, 56, *56*
Brady Bill, 56
Brandenburg Gate, 78, *79*
Brother Rat, 22
Brown, Edmund G. (Pat), 32, 36–37, 38
Bush, George H. W., 45, 58, *66*, *68*, 77, 80,
        82, 83, 90, *91*
Bush, George W., 90, *91*

campaigns and elections
    for California governor, 1962, 32
    for California governor, 1966, 35–38, *37*
    for president of the U.S., 1948–1964, 32,
        33, 34
    for president of the U.S., 1976, 42–43, *44*
    for president of the U.S., 1980, 45, *46*,
        47–49
    for president of the U.S., 1984, 65–67, *66*,
        68, 69, *70*
    for president of the U.S., 1988, *82*, 83
Carter, Jimmy, 43, 47–49, 52, 90, *91*
Central Intelligence Agency, 61

Challenger space shuttle, 72, *72*
Chernenko, Konstantin, 73
Christopher, George, 36
Cleaver, Margaret "Mugs," 13, 15
Clinton, Bill, 90, *91*, 92
Communism, 26–27, 37, 60–62, 78, 80
Contras, 61–62, 75–77
Cuba, 62

Dark Victory, 21
Davis, Nancy. *See* Reagan, Nancy Davis
D-Day, 64
debates in presidential campaign, *68*, 69
Democratic party, 31–32, 66, 67, 71
Dole, Robert, 45
domestic policy, 40–41, 58, 59–60, 71
Dow Jones Industrial Average, 80
Dukakis, Michael, 83

economy
    California, late 1960s, 40
    Great Depression, 1930s, 16–17
    national, late 1970s, 47
    national, 1980s, 57–60
    Reaganomics, 57–60
    stock market crash, 1987, 80, *81*
Eisenhower, Dwight D., 32, 37
elections. *See* campaigns and elections
Eureka College, 13, 15–16

Falwell, Jerry, 67
fast facts
    Nancy Reagan, 97
    Ronald Reagan, 92
    World War II, 25
Ferraro, Geraldine, 66–67, *68*
Ford, Gerald, 42–43, *44*, 90, *91*

foreign policy, 60–64, 73, 75–78, 80
Foster, Jody, 56
Fulks, Sarah Jane. *See* Wyman, Jane

General Electric Theater, 29, 31
Gipp, George, 22, *23*
Goldwater, Barry, 32, 67
Gorbachev, Mikhail, 73, *74*, 75, 78, 80, 90
governor's mansion, 39
Great Depression, 16–17
Grenada, 62

Haig, Alexander, 52
Hinckley, John, Jr., 55–56
Hodges, Joy, 18
Holden, William and Ardis, 29, *30*
hostages (U.S.) in Iran, 47, 49, 52, *53*
HUAC (House Un-American Activities
        Committee), 26–27

Iran-Contra Affair, 75–77. *See also* Contras

John Birch Society, 37
Johnny Belinda, 24
Johnson, Lyndon B., 32

Kennedy, John F., 32
Knute Rockne All American, 22, *23*

Lebanon, 62–64
Love Is On the Air, 21

Martin, Dean, 38
McAuliffe, Christa, 72
Meese, Edwin, III, 52
Meiklejohn, Bill, 18–19
Mondale, Walter, 66–67, 69
Moral Majority, 67
movie industry, 21–22, 24–29

New Right movement, 67
New York Stock Exchange, 80, *81*
Nicaragua, 61–62, 75–77
Nixon, Richard, 32, *42*, 43
Normandy, France, 64
North, Oliver, 76, 77
nuclear arms, 73, 75

Poindexter, John M., 76, 77

radio, 17–18
Reagan, John Edward "Jack", 9, *10*, 11, 13, 16
Reagan, Maureen, 24, 90
Reagan, Michael, 28, 90
Reagan, Nancy Davis, *44*, *55*, *63*
    children, 31
    courtship and marriage, 28–29, *30*
    first lady, 88
    governor's mansion, 39
    retirement, 89–90
Reagan, Neil, 9, *10*, 11, 15
Reagan, Nelle Wilson, 9, *10*, 12, 16
Reagan, Patti, 31, 90
Reagan, Ronald, Jr., 31, 90
Reagan, Ronald Wilson, *44*, *46*, *93*
    assassination attempt, 7, 9, 54–56
    author, 86
    birth and childhood, 9, *10*, 11
    children, 24, 28, 31
    courtship/marriage to Jane Wyman, 22, 24,
        24, 28
    courtship/marriage to Nancy Davis, 28–29,
        30
    death and funeral service, 90, *91*
    education, 11–13, 15–17
    governor of California, *39*, 39–41, *42*
    health, 71, 87–90
    host of *General Electric Theater*, 29, 31, *31*
    inauguration, 51–52

Reagan, Ronald Wilson (cont'd.)
    lifeguard, 13, *14*, 17
    military career, 25
    modern views on, 92, 94–95
    movie and television actor, 18–19, 21–22,
        23, *24*, 24–29, 31, *31*
    newspaper columnist, 41–42, 43
    nicknames, 9, 22, 77
    president of U.S., 1st term, *8*, 54–64, *55*,
        56, *58*
    president of U.S., 2nd term, 65–67, *66*, 69,
        70, 71, 73, *74*, 75–78, *79*, 80, *82*, 83
    president of Screen Actors Guild (SAG),
        25–29, *27*
    public speaker, 87
    radio announcer, *17*, 17–18
    retirement, 85, *86*, 87
    summer jobs, 13, *14*
Reaganomics, 57–60
Reagan Revolution, 58–59, 80, 83, 92
Republican party, 31–32, 35, 41, 43, 45, 65,
    69, 71
Robbins, Anne Frances. *See* Reagan, Nancy
    Davis

Sandinistas, 61
Schroeder, Patricia, 77
Screen Actors Guild (SAG), 25–27
Sinatra, Frank, 38
Social Security, 92
Soviet Union, 60–61, 73, 75, 78, 80
space shuttle *Challenger*, 72, *72*

Star Wars. *See* Strategic Defense Initiative
stock market/stock traders, 80, *81*
Strategic Defense Initiative (Star Wars),
    60–61, 75

taxes, tax code and laws, 58, 71
television, 29, 31
terrorism/terrorists, 47, 49, 52, 62–64
Thatcher, Margaret, 90
timeline, 98–99
Treaty on the Elimination of Intermediate-
    Range and Shorter Range Nuclear
    Forces (INF), 75
Truman, Harry, 31

unions, 25–27
U.S. embassy, Beirut, 62–64
U.S. embassy, Tehran, 47, 49, 52
U.S. military
    defense spending, 58–59, 60
    Marine barracks bombing, *63*, 63–64
    Star Wars missile defense system, 75
    Strategic Defense Initiative (SDI), 60–61

Wall Street, 80
Warner Brothers, 19
Wayne, John, 38
Weinberger, Caspar, 52
welfare reform, 40–41, 59–60
White House, 54
World War II, 25, 64
Wyman, Jane, 22, 24, *24*, 28

About the Author

Kieran Doherty is the award-winning author of fourteen books for young readers. A career journalist and magazine writer before turning his attention to writing for children and teens, he particularly enjoys writing historical nonfiction. Doherty, an avid sailor, lives in Lake Worth, Florida, with his wife, Lynne.